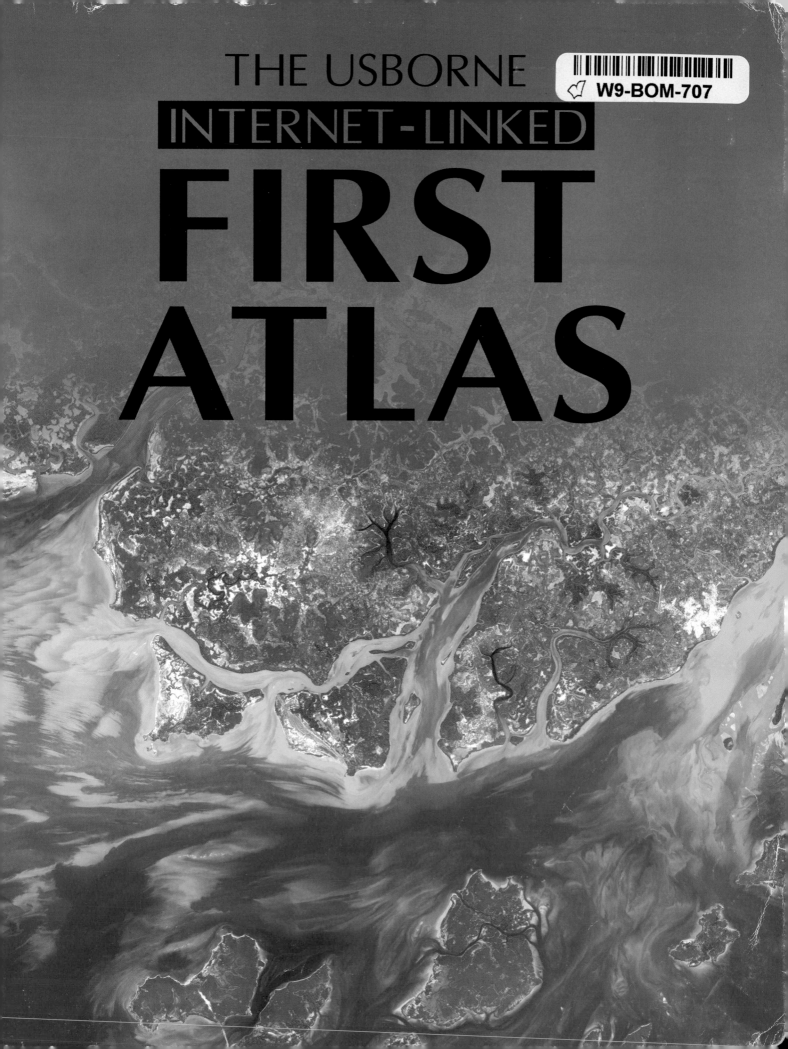

THE USBORNE
INTERNET-LINKED
FIRST ATLAS

First published in 2003 by Usborne Publishing Ltd,
Usborne House, 83–85 Saffron Hill, London EC1N 8RT, England.

www.usborne.com

Printed in Portugal

Title page: A satellite image showing rivers joining the sea, along the coast of
Guinea-Bissau in west Africa. The red parts are land and the blue parts are water.
This page: These mountains and glaciers are on the island of Svalbard, which belongs
to Norway. The island is far inside the Arctic Circle and it's very cold there.

THE USBORNE
INTERNET-LINKED
FIRST ATLAS

Elizabeth Dalby

Designed by Laura Hammonds,
Candice Whatmore and Ruth Russell

Additional design: Adam Constantine, Michael Hill,
Karen Tomlins, Joanne Kirkby and Luke Sargent

Digital imagery by Keith Furnival

Edited by Kirsteen Rogers

Cover design: Zöe Wray

Cartography: European Map Graphics Ltd

Consultant: John Davidson

Consultant cartographic editor: Craig Asquith

Website adviser: Lisa Watts

912
DALBY, E

Internet links

There are lots of exciting places on the Internet where you can find out more about the different countries, customs, people and animals in this book. The "Internet link" boxes in this book contain descriptions of websites you can visit by clicking on links on the Usborne Quicklinks Website.

Just go to **www.usborne-quicklinks.com** and enter the keywords "first atlas". Here are some of the things you can do on the websites described in this book:

- Find exciting games and activities from Africa
- Discover the creatures living on a coral reef
- Visit the Eiffel Tower
- Build a virtual rice paddy
- Take an Arctic quiz

Safety on the Internet

Here are a few simple rules to help keep you safe while you are online:

- Ask your parent's or guardian's permission before you connect to the Internet.
- Never give out information such as your real name, address or telephone number.
- Never arrange to meet someone you started talking to on the Internet.
- If a site asks you to log in or register by typing your name or email address, ask permission from an adult first.
- If you receive an email from someone you don't know, tell an adult. Don't reply to it.

Site availability

The links in Usborne Quicklinks are regularly updated, but occasionally, you may get a message that a site is unavailable. This might be temporary, so try again later. If any of the sites close down, we will, if possible, replace them with alternatives. You will find an up-to-date list of sites at Usborne Quicklinks.

What you need

Most of the websites listed in this book can be accessed using a standard home computer and a web browser (the software that lets you look at information from the Internet). Some sites need extra programs (plug-ins) to play sound or show videos or animations. If you go to a site and do not have the necessary plug-in, a message will come up on the screen. There is usually a button on the site that you can click on to download the plug-in. Alternatively, go to **www.usborne-quicklinks.com** and click on Net Help. There, you can find links to download plug-ins.

Notes for parents

The websites described in this book are regularly reviewed and the links in Usborne Quicklinks are updated. However, the content of a website may change at any time and Usborne Publishing is not responsible for the content on any website other than its own. We recommend that children are supervised while on the Internet, that they do not use Internet Chat Rooms, and that you use Internet filtering software to block unsuitable material. Please ensure that your children read and follow the safety guidelines printed in the box on the left. For more information, see the Net Help area on the Usborne Quicklinks Website.

www.usborne-quicklinks.com

Go to **www.usborne-quicklinks.com** and enter the keywords "first atlas" for direct links to all the websites in this book.

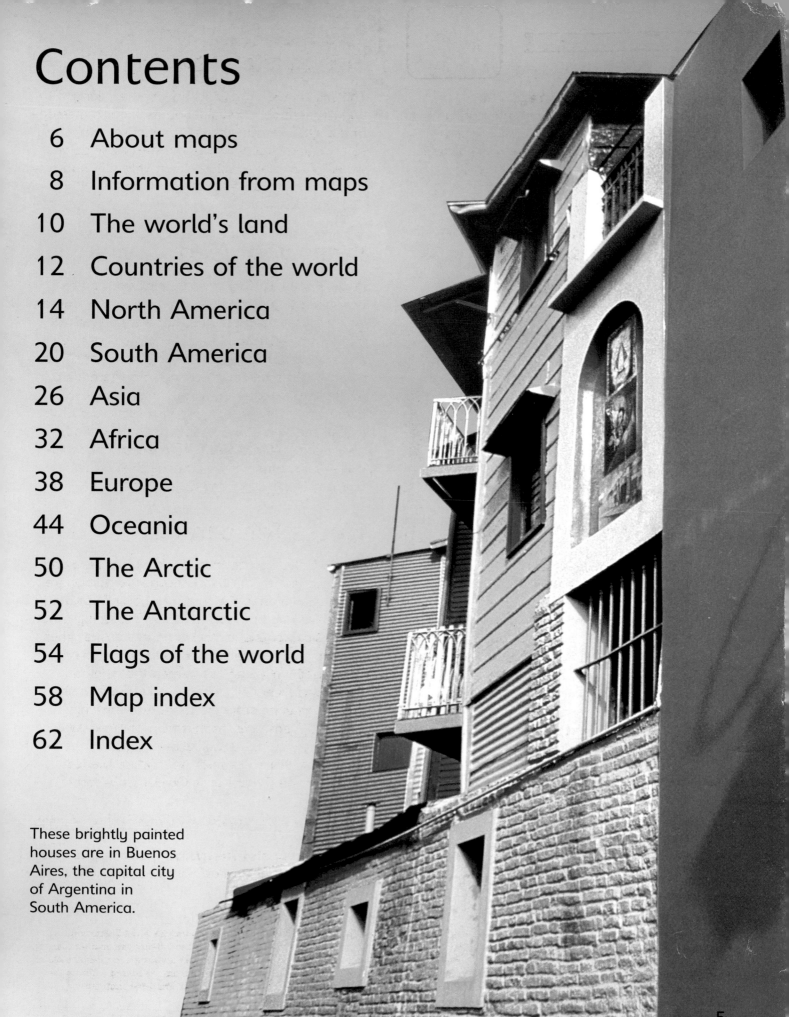

Contents

These brightly painted houses are in Buenos Aires, the capital city of Argentina in South America.

About maps

An atlas is a collection of maps. Maps are pictures of areas, seen from above. They show places much smaller than they really are. Some maps show the whole world, and some show much smaller areas, like cities or streets.

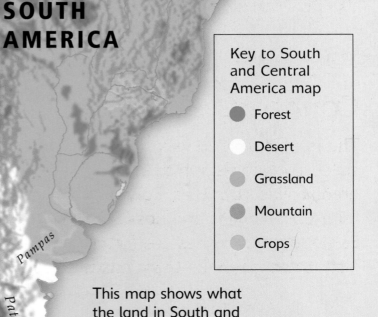

What will you see on a map?

Maps should be easy to understand. Different kinds of shading and symbols help show what a place is like. A key explains what they all mean.

The size of a map compared with the real-life area it shows is called its scale. Some maps have a line called a scale bar that shows you the real distances between places on the map.

Which way is up?

The Earth doesn't really have a top and a bottom. Maps are often drawn with north at the top, though, to make them easier for everyone to understand.

Key to South and Central America map

- Forest
- Desert
- Grassland
- Mountain
- Crops

This map shows what the land in South and Central America is like.

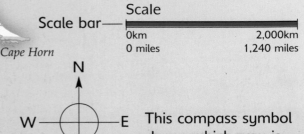

Scale bar

Scale

0km — 2,000km
0 miles — 1,240 miles

This compass symbol shows which way is north (N), south (S), east (E) and west (W).

Sea and land

More than two-thirds of the Earth is covered in salty water – the seas and oceans. Maps usually show water in blue.

The rest of the Earth is covered in land. Maps sometimes shade the land as it would look from above. Grasslands are often green and deserts can be sandy brown or yellow.

An island is land with water all around it. This is one of the Solomon Islands, in the Pacific Ocean.

Countries and continents

The land is divided into seven huge areas called continents, which are split into smaller areas called countries. Each country is run by a government and has its own laws. Some large countries are further divided into states, to make them easier to run.

Internet link

For links to websites where you can play games about countries and continents, go to **www.usborne-quicklinks.com**

This is the continent of North America. It is a large area of land and islands.

North America is divided into countries, including Canada, the USA and Mexico.

The USA is divided into 50 different states. Each state can make its own laws.

Information from maps

Maps can show different things about the same area. Some maps show where countries and cities are. Some show what the land looks like or what kinds of plants grow there.

Political maps show countries and place names. The lines between countries are called borders or boundaries.

Physical maps show what the land looks like. They show features like mountains, lakes and rivers.

Thematic maps show other information, such as what the land is used for, or how many people live there.

Weather and wildlife

Different parts of the world have their own weather patterns, plants and wildlife. These areas are called biomes. Deserts, grasslands and rainforests are biomes. They can all be shown on a thematic map.

These cacti live in the desert, where it hardly ever rains. They store water in their stems.

Internet link

For links to websites with fun games about maps, go to **www.usborne-quicklinks.com**

How many people?

The people who live in an area are its population. Maps can be used to show which parts of an area are crowded, and which parts have very few people living in them.

This map of North America shows the areas where most people live.

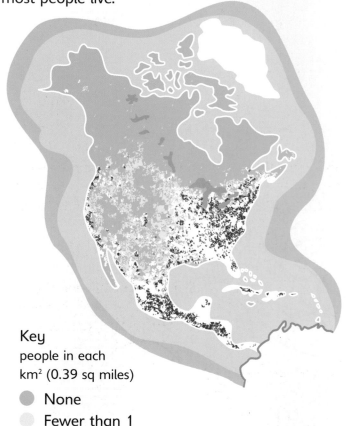

Key
people in each
km² (0.39 sq miles)

- None
- Fewer than 1
- Up to 100
- More than 100

Towns and cities

Anywhere where a group of people live is called a settlement. A village is a small settlement, a town is bigger, and the largest kind is a city. The capital city of a country is where its government is based. About half the people in the world live in a town or a city.

Lines on maps

To make it easy to measure distances and find places on a map, the Earth is divided up with imaginary lines. The two sets of lines are called longitude and latitude. They are numbered in degrees (°) and minutes (´).

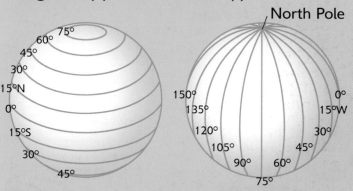

Lines of latitude run around the globe. On maps they usually run from left to right.

Longitude lines run from the North to the South Pole, and usually from top to bottom on maps.

This drawing of the Earth shows the North Pole and the main lines of longitude and latitude.

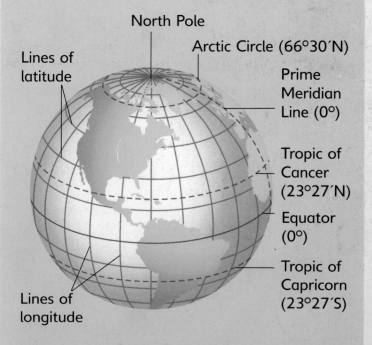

This globe is tipped slightly forward so the North Pole shows. This means that you can't quite see the South Pole.

The world's land

This is a physical map. It shows the different kinds of land in each continent.

The top half of the globe is called the northern hemisphere.

The bottom half of the globe is called the southern hemisphere.

Beaufort Sea
Victoria Island
Queen Elizabeth Islands
Ellesmere Island
Greenland
Greenland S
Baffin Island
Baffin Bay
Iceland
Arctic Circle
Alaska
Mount McKinley
Mackenzie
Great Bear Lake
Hudson Bay
Labrador Sea
British Isles
Aleutian Islands
Gulf of Alaska
Rocky Mountains
Yukon
NORTH AMERICA
Missouri
Lake Superior
Lake Huron
Newfoundland
Great Plains
Lake Michigan
Appalachian Mountains
Azores
Rio Grande
Mississippi
Atlas Mount
Tropic of Cancer
Hawaiian Islands
Gulf of Mexico
Canary Islands
Sah
20° N
Central America
Cuba
West Indies
Cape Verde Islands
Niger
Caribbean Sea
PACIFIC
Galapagos Islands
Guiana Highlands
ATLANTIC
Equator
OCEAN
Amazon
OCEAN
Amazon Rainforest
Polynesia
SOUTH AMERICA
Andes
Tahiti
Atacama Desert
20° S
Tropic of Capricorn
Easter Island
Aconcagua
Parana
Pampas
40°
Patagonia
Falkland Islands
South Georgia
Cape Horn
Drake Passage
60°
Antarctic Circle
Antarctic Peninsula
Weddell Sea
80
Vinson Massif

Key to map of the world's land

- Forest
- Grassland
- Desert
- Mountain (only high mountains are shown)
- Tundra areas (frozen ground with no trees)
- Ice (areas where the ice or snow never melts)
- Crops (land used for growing plants for people and animals to eat)
- Sea
- Lake or inland sea
- River
- ▲ Mountain peak

ARCTIC OCEAN

40° 60° 80° 100° 120° 140° 160° 180° 80°

Severnaya Zemlya
Novaya Zemlya
Svalbard
North Cape
Kara Sea
Laptev Sea
New Siberia Islands
East Siberian Sea
Barents Sea
Scandinavia

Arctic Circle

Siberia
60°
Ob
Yenisey
Verkhoyansk Range
Lena
Sea of Okhotsk
Bering Sea
Kamchatka Peninsula

EUROPE
Volga
Ural Mountains
Lake Baikal
Amur
Danube
Mount Elbrus ▲
Black Sea
Caspian Sea
Aral Sea
Altai Mountains
ASIA
Gobi Desert
Sea of Japan
Japan
40°

Mediterranean Sea
Indus
Himalayas
Yellow
Honshu
China
East China Sea

Libyan Desert
Nile
Arabia
Red Sea
Ganges
Mount Everest ▲
Yangtze
Taiwan
PACIFIC
Tropic of Cancer

Desert
Rub al Khali (Empty Quarter)
Arabian Sea
India
Bay of Bengal
Mekong
Luzon
Philippines
Micronesia
OCEAN
20° N

Sahel
Ethiopian Highlands
Cape Comorin
Sri Lanka
South China Sea
Mindanao

AFRICA
Lake Victoria
Seychelles
Borneo
Celebes
New Guinea
Melanesia
Equator 0°

Kilimanjaro ▲
INDIAN
Sumatra
Java Sea
Mount Wilhelm ▲
Solomon Islands

Comoro Islands
OCEAN
Java
Arafura Sea
Coral Sea
Fiji Islands

Zambezi
Madagascar
Mauritius
Great Sandy Desert
Great Barrier Reef
New Caledonia
20° S
Tropic of Capricorn

OCEANIA
Great Dividing Range

Cape of Good Hope
Great Victoria Desert
Tasman Sea
North Island
40°

Kerguelen Islands
Tasmania
South Island

60°

SOUTHERN OCEAN
Antarctic Circle

ANTARCTICA
Ross Sea
80°

40° 60° 80° 100° 120° 140° 160° 180°

Scale

0km ———————— 3,000km
0 miles   1,860 miles

11

Countries of the world

This is a political map. It shows the different countries that make up each continent. Can you find your country on the map?

ALASKA (U.S.A.)

Arctic Circle

GREENLAND (Denmark)

ICELAND

CANADA

UNITED KINGDOM

IRELAND

DE

B

UNITED STATES OF AMERICA

FRA

SPAIN

Azores (Portugal)

PORTUGAL

MOROCCO

Canary Islands (Spain)

ALGE

WESTERN SAHARA (Morocco)

Tropic of Cancer

THE BAHAMAS

MEXICO

CUBA

DOMINICAN REPUBLIC

HAITI

JAMAICA

DOMINICA

MAURITANIA

MALI

Hawaiian Islands (U.S.A.)

BELIZE

HONDURAS

Caribbean Sea

CAPE VERDE

SENEGAL

GUATEMALA

NICARAGUA

THE GAMBIA

BURKINA FASO

EL SALVADOR

GUINEA-BISSAU

GUINEA

COSTA RICA

TRINIDAD AND TOBAGO

SIERRA LEONE

IVORY COAST

TOGO

PANAMA

VENEZUELA

GUYANA

LIBERIA

GHANA

EQUA

SURINAM

COLOMBIA

FRENCH GUIANA (France)

SAO TOME AND PRINCIPE

PACIFIC

Galapagos Islands (Ecuador)

ECUADOR

ATLANTIC

KIRIBATI

OCEAN

PERU

BRAZIL

OCEAN

Cook Islands (New Zealand)

BOLIVIA

French Polynesia (France)

Tropic of Capricorn

Pitcairn Islands (U.K.)

PARAGUAY

CHILE

URUGUAY

ARGENTINA

Falkland Islands (U.K.)

South Georgia (U.K.)

Antarctic Circle

SOUTHE

Weddell Sea

Equator

Key to map of countries of the world

— Border, where one country is joined to the next one

— Coast

Lake or inland sea

Some country names had to be shortened to fit on the map. This list has the names written in full.

ARM.	Armenia
AUST.	Austria
AZER.	Azerbaijan
BELG.	Belgium
B.H.	Boznia and Herzegovina
CRO.	Croatia
CZECH REP.	Czech Republic
LEB.	Lebanon
LUX.	Luxembourg
MAC.	Macedonia
NETH.	Netherlands
SLOV.	Slovenia
S.M.	Serbia and Montenegro
SWITZ.	Switzerland
U.A.E	United Arab Emirates

Scale

0km   3,000km
0 miles   1,860 miles

ARCTIC OCEAN

RUSSIA

FINLAND
ESTONIA
LATVIA
LITHUANIA
BELARUS
UKRAINE
MOLDOVA
ROMANIA
BULGARIA
Black Sea
GREECE
TURKEY
CYPRUS
LEB.
SYRIA
ISRAEL
JORDAN
IRAQ
KUWAIT

KAZAKHSTAN
UZBEKISTAN
TURKMENISTAN
TAJIKISTAN
KYRGYZSTAN
GEORGIA
ARM. AZER.
Caspian Sea

MONGOLIA

CHINA

NORTH KOREA
SOUTH KOREA
JAPAN

PACIFIC OCEAN

IRAN
AFGHANISTAN
PAKISTAN
NEPAL
BHUTAN
BANGLA-DESH
BURMA (MYANMAR)
LAOS
THAILAND
VIETNAM
CAMBODIA

BAHRAIN
QATAR
U.A.E.
OMAN

SAUDI ARABIA

INDIA

TAIWAN

Tropic of Cancer

20° N

LIBYA
EGYPT

SUDAN

CENTRAL AFRICAN REPUBLIC
CHAD

ERITREA
DJIBOUTI
ETHIOPIA
SOMALIA
YEMEN

SRI LANKA

MALDIVES

PHILIPPINES

Northern Mariana Islands (U.S.A.)

MARSHALL ISLANDS

PALAU

FEDERATED STATES OF MICRONESIA

BRUNEI
MALAYSIA
SINGAPORE

INDONESIA

NAURU

KIRIBATI

Equator 0°

CONGO (DEMOCRATIC REPUBLIC)
UGANDA
RWANDA
BURUNDI
KENYA
TANZANIA

SEYCHELLES

INDIAN OCEAN

PAPUA NEW GUINEA

SOLOMON ISLANDS

TUVALU

ANGOLA
ZAMBIA
MALAWI
COMOROS

EAST TIMOR

SAMOA

ZIMBABWE
MADAGASCAR
MAURITIUS
Reunion (France)

Coral Sea Islands Territory (Australia)

VANUATU
New Caledonia (France)

FIJI
TONGA

20° S

BOTSWANA
MOZAMBIQUE
SWAZILAND
SOUTH AFRICA
LESOTHO

Tropic of Capricorn

AUSTRALIA

40°

OCEAN

Kerguelen Islands (France)

NEW ZEALAND

60°

Antarctic Circle

ANTARCTICA

80°

13

North America

This continent includes three huge countries – Canada, the USA and Mexico. It also includes the Caribbean islands and the countries in the strip of land that joins onto South America.

Key to North America map

- ■ Capital city
- ○ Major city or town
- ― Border (where one country joins another one)
- ― River
- ▬ Coast

PACIFIC OCEAN

Scale

0km	1,000km
0 miles	620 miles

ARCTIC OCEAN

Queen Elizabeth Islands

Parry Isla

Point Barrow

Beaufort Sea

Victoria Island

ALASKA (U.S.A.)

Bering Strait

Bering Sea

Yukon

Mount McKinley ▲

Anchorage ○

Great Bear Lake

Mackenzie

Gulf of Alaska

Great Slave Lake

CANA

Lake Athabas

Reindeer Lake

ROCKY MOUNTAINS

Vancouver ○

Calgary ○

Great Plains

Win

Seattle ○

Columbia

California

Great Salt Lake

UNITED STATE (U

San Francisco ○

Colorado

Denver ○

Los Angeles ○

Phoenix ○

Ciudad Juarez ○

Te.

Hawaiian Islands (U.S.A.)

Lower California

Hermosillo ○

Rio

Tropic of Cancer

Monterrey

MEXIC

Guadala

Mexico Cit

Acapulco

Raccoons live in North and Central America. They usually sleep in trees during the day and come out at night to feed.

Arctic Circle

Internet link

For links to websites where you can print out maps and take virtual tours of North American countries, go to **www.usborne-quicklinks.com**

14

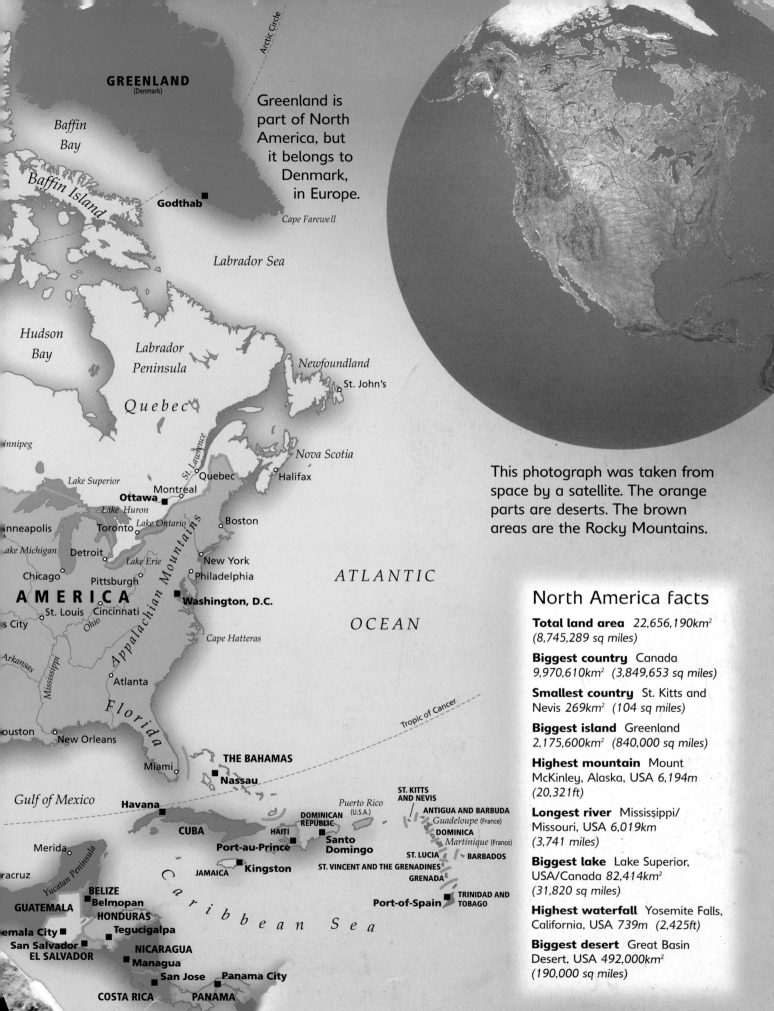

GREENLAND
(Denmark)

Baffin Bay

Baffin Island

Godthab ■

Greenland is part of North America, but it belongs to Denmark, in Europe.

Cape Farewell

Labrador Sea

Hudson Bay

Labrador Peninsula

Newfoundland

innipeg

Quebec

St. John's

St. Lawrence

Quebec

Nova Scotia

Montreal ○

Halifax

Ottawa ○

Lake Superior

Lake Huron

Lake Ontario

Toronto ○

Boston ○

nneapolis

Detroit ○

Lake Erie

ke Michigan

Chicago ○

Pittsburgh ○

New York ○

Philadelphia ○

A M E R I C A

St. Louis ○

Cincinnati ○

Ohio

Appalachian Mountains

■ **Washington, D.C.**

s City

Arkansas

Atlanta ○

Cape Hatteras

Mississippi

Florida

ouston

New Orleans ○

Miami ○

Gulf of Mexico

Havana ●

Merida ○

acruz

Yucatan Peninsula

BELIZE

Belmopan ■

GUATEMALA

HONDURAS

emala City ■

Tegucigalpa ■

San Salvador ■

EL SALVADOR

NICARAGUA

Managua ■

San Jose ■

COSTA RICA

Panama City ●

PANAMA

THE BAHAMAS

● **Nassau**

Tropic of Cancer

Puerto Rico (U.S.A.)

DOMINICAN REPUBLIC

CUBA

HAITI

Port-au-Prince ●

Santo Domingo ●

JAMAICA

Kingston ●

Caribbean Sea

ST. KITTS AND NEVIS

ANTIGUA AND BARBUDA

Guadeloupe (France)

DOMINICA

Martinique (France)

ST. LUCIA

● **BARBADOS**

ST. VINCENT AND THE GRENADINES

GRENADA

Port-of-Spain ■

TRINIDAD AND TOBAGO

A T L A N T I C

O C E A N

Arctic Circle

This photograph was taken from space by a satellite. The orange parts are deserts. The brown areas are the Rocky Mountains.

North America facts

Total land area 22,656,190km² (8,745,289 sq miles)

Biggest country Canada 9,970,610km² (3,849,653 sq miles)

Smallest country St. Kitts and Nevis 269km² (104 sq miles)

Biggest island Greenland 2,175,600km² (840,000 sq miles)

Highest mountain Mount McKinley, Alaska, USA 6,194m (20,321ft)

Longest river Mississippi/ Missouri, USA 6,019km (3,741 miles)

Biggest lake Lake Superior, USA/Canada 82,414km² (31,820 sq miles)

Highest waterfall Yosemite Falls, California, USA 739m (2,425ft)

Biggest desert Great Basin Desert, USA 492,000km² (190,000 sq miles)

15

Using the land

Much of the land in North America is hard to live and work on. Some areas are hot and rocky, and some are freezing and snowy. In other parts of North America, the land and weather are just right for farming.

Shapes in the rock

In the southwest USA, some of the rocky land has slowly been worn away by rivers to make channels called canyons. Strong winds and rain have worn the rock away even more, making strange, rippling shapes.

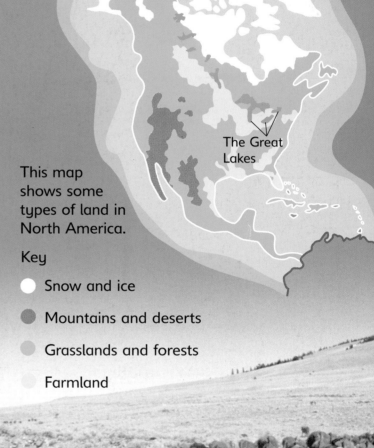

The Great Lakes

This map shows some types of land in North America.

Key

● Snow and ice

● Mountains and deserts

● Grasslands and forests

● Farmland

This strange photograph shows part of a small canyon in Arizona. The orange rock is called sandstone and the big cat is a puma.

Shaking ground

The Earth's crust is made up of huge slabs of rock, called plates. Sometimes they push or slide against each other, making the ground shake. This is called an earthquake. The San Andreas Fault, in the west of the USA, is a place where two plates slide past each other. Earthquakes often happen there.

This house fell down after a big earthquake in San Francisco, a city on the San Andreas Fault.

Massive farms

In the USA, Canada and Mexico, there are many huge cattle farms, called ranches. The cattle are farmed for their meat and skins. Other farms in North America grow crops such as corn and vegetables in enormous fields.

Internet link

For a link to a website with a clickable map and photographs of the biggest canyon in the world, go to **www.usborne-quicklinks.com**

One of the best ways for cowboys to move around their land and round up cattle is on horseback. Some farms are so big it would take days to walk across them.

Cities and celebrations

Explorers from Europe arrived in North America a few hundred years ago. But people have lived there for many thousands of years. Today, people come from all over the world to live there.

Stone cities

The Maya and the Aztec people lived in Mexico before European settlers came. The Maya built beautiful cities and pyramid-shaped temples out of stone. Ruins of these can still be seen today, on the Yucatan Peninsula in Mexico.

This map shows where some early North American people lived.

Key

- Aztecs
- Maya
- Native American tribes

Inuit
Inuit
Chipewyan
Cree
Inuit
Cree
Blackfoot
Chippewa
Huron
Chinook
Crow
Cheyenne
Cherokee
Sioux
Iroquois
Comanche
Hopi
Navajo
Creek
Chickshaw
Chocktaw
Apache
Yucatan Peninsula

This Mayan temple is over 1,000 years old.

The Maya believed their kings were gods and built temples like this one to worship them.

Busy city

New York City is the biggest city in the USA, and also one of the largest cities in the world. Almost 20 million people live there, and thousands more visit every year.

Internet link

For links to websites where you can find out more about the peoples of North America, go to **www.usborne-quicklinks.com**

Part of New York is on an island called Manhattan. Bridges join Manhattan to the rest of the city.

Icy homeland

Inuit people live in the icy north of Canada, in an area called Nunavut. It's too cold to grow crops there, so Inuit hunters catch animals and fish for people to eat.

This Inuit man is making a harpoon spear to take hunting. He is wearing warm fur clothes.

Calypso music

People visit the Caribbean islands for warm weather and sandy beaches. The islands are also famous for calypso music, which people play on drums made out of old oil cans.

This girl is dressed for Trinidad's carnival. Dancing and music are an important part of the celebrations.

South America

South America stretches down from the equator almost as far as the Antarctic. It is joined to North America by a narrow strip of land at the edge of Colombia.

Key to South America map

- ■ Capital city
- ○ Major city or town
- ▦ Border (where one country joins another one)
- — River
- ▬ Coast

Scale

0km	1,000km
0 miles	620 miles

Caribbean Sea

○ Maracaibo   ■ **Caracas**

VENEZUELA

○ Medellin

■ **Bogota**   *Guiana Highle*

○ Cali   **COLOMBIA**   *Orinoco*

Equator

Galapagos Islands (Ecuador)

■ **Quito**   *Negro*

ECUADOR   *Amazon*

○ Guayaquil

Amazon Rainfore

PERU

Ucayali

A N D E S

■ **Lima**

Lake Titicaca   **BOLIVIA**

■ **La Paz**

■ **Sucre**

Atacama Desert

Tropic of Capricorn

PACIFIC

OCEAN

CHILE   ○ San Mig de Tucu

A N D E S

○ Cordoba

▲ *Aconcagua*   Ro

■ **Santiago**

ARGENTIN

Pam

Patagonia

This is a toucan. Toucans live in South American rainforests. They use their long beaks to pick and eat fruit from the trees.

Strait of Mage

Tierra del F

Cape Horn

Drake Pas

orgetown

Paramaribo

Cayenne

NA

RINAM

FRENCH
GUIANA
(France)

Reservoir *Amazon*

Equator

Belem

Xingu

Tucurui Reservoir

Fortaleza

Tocantins

B R A Z I L

*Sobradinho
Reservoir*

Recife

*Plateau of
Mato Grosso*

São Francisco

Brazilian Highlands

Salvador

Brasilia

Goiania

Belo Horizonte

Parana

*Furnas
Reservoir*

Rio de Janeiro

GUAY

Sao Paulo

Tropic of Capricorn

Asuncion

Curitiba

Porto Alegre

ATLANTIC

OCEAN

UGUAY

Montevideo

nos Aires

d Islands
(U.K.)

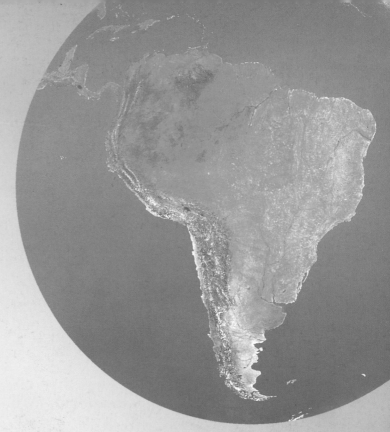

This is what South America looks like from space. The mottled strip along the west coast shows the Andes Mountains.

South America facts

Total land area *17,866,130km²
(6,898,113 sq miles)*

Biggest country Brazil *8,547,400km²
(3,300,151 sq miles)*

Smallest country Surinam *163,270km²
(63,039 sq miles)*

Biggest island Tierra del Fuego *46,360km²
(17,900 sq miles)*

Highest mountain Aconcagua, Argentina
6,959m (22,831ft)

Longest river Amazon, Brazil *6,440km
(4,000 miles)*

Biggest lake Lake Maracaibo, Venezuela
13,312km² (5,140 sq miles)

Highest waterfall Angel Falls,
on the Churun River, Venezuela
979m (3,212ft)

Biggest desert Patagonian Desert,
Argentina *673,000km²
(260,000 sq miles)*

Internet link

For links to websites where you can print out maps and take virtual tours of South America, go to **www.usborne-quicklinks.com**

21

Wettest and driest

South America has one of the wettest places on Earth in it – the Amazon Rainforest. But it also has the Atacama Desert, which is one of the driest. South America's Andes Mountains make up the the longest chain of mountains in the world.

Snowy peaks

The Andes Mountains are over 7,000km (4,300 miles) long, and stretch all the way down the continent. The lower slopes are good for farming, but the high peaks are snowy and bleak. More than 30 of the peaks in the Andes are volcanoes.

This map shows some of the landscape features of South America.

This climber is close to the top of Huascaran, one of the highest peaks in the Andes.

Key

- Amazon Rainforest
- Rivers in the Amazon
- Atacama Desert
- Andes Mountains

Forest homes

The Amazon Rainforest is the biggest rainforest in the world. It's always hot there and it rains nearly every day. The forest is home to a huge number of plants and animals.

This blue morpho butterfly comes from the Amazon. It's as big as a man's hand.

Internet link

For links to websites where you can explore the Amazon River and find lots of animal facts, go to **www.usborne-quicklinks.com**

Dry ground

The Atacama Desert, in Chile, is next to the Pacific Ocean but it is the driest place on the planet. In some parts of the desert, people think it may never have rained at all.

Desert plants like these have long roots to reach way down into the cracked earth for water.

Mighty river

There's more water in the Amazon River than in any other river in the world. Over 1,000 smaller rivers flow into it, from all over the north part of South America. It is also one of the longest rivers, and winds nearly all the way across the top of the continent.

This boy is paddling his boat along the Amazon River. The main part of the river is so wide there are no bridges over it.

23

Places for living

South Americans live high in the mountains, deep in the rainforest, and even in the desert. Many people live in tiny farming villages, but South America also has some of the biggest cities in the world.

This map shows the places where most people live in South America.

Key
people in each km²
(0.39 sq miles)

- None
- Fewer than 1
- Up to 100
- More than 100

The Uros people use boats made of reeds to cross Lake Titicaca.

Mountain lake

Lake Titicaca is high up in the Andes Mountains, near Peru and Bolivia. The Uros people live by the lake and go fishing in its icy waters. Some of them live on floating islands made of reeds.

Mysterious statues

Easter Island, in the Pacific Ocean, is covered in hundreds of stone figures called *moai*. They were made by the first people who lived there, to worship their ancestors.

Most *moai* statues are at least twice the height of a man, and very heavy. How they were moved into place is a mystery.

City celebration

Early every year, the busy city of Rio de Janeiro in Brazil holds a carnival. It lasts for five days, with feasting, music and costume parades. Dancers take part in samba competitions across the city.

At carnival time in Rio de Janeiro, floats like this one carry costumed people through the streets of the city.

Internet link

For links to websites about the celebrations, music and people of South America, go to **www.usborne-quicklinks.com**

Asia

Asia is the biggest continent. It stretches from the Arctic Circle to the equator, and from the Ural Mountains in the west to the Pacific Ocean in the east.

The part of Russia on this side of the Ural Mountains is in Europe.

Key to Asia map

■ Capital city
○ Major city or town
▬ Border (where one country joins another one)
― River
▬ Coast

Scale

0km   1,000km
0 miles   640 miles

ARCTIC OCEAN

Novaya Zemlya
Barents Sea
Kara Sea
Arctic Circle

St. Petersburg
Arkhangelsk
Ural Mountains
Ob
Yenisey
No

Moscow
Nizhniy Novgorod
Kazan
Yekaterinburg
Irtysh
Omsk
Novosibirs
R U S

Volga
Samara
Chelyabinsk
Aqtobe
Altai Mou

Istanbul
Rostov
Astrakhan
Caspian Sea
KAZAKHSTAN
Astana

Izmir
Ankara
Black Sea
Caucasus Mountains
Aral Sea
Lake Balkhash

TURKEY
GEORGIA
Tbilisi
ARMENIA
Yerevan
AZERBAIJAN
Baku
Tabriz
UZBEKISTAN
Almaty
Urumc

CYPRUS
Nicosia
TURKMENISTAN
Ashgabat
Tashkent
Bishkek
KYRGYZSTAN

Beirut
LEBANON
SYRIA
Damascus
Tigris
Dushanbe
TAJIKISTAN

ISRAEL
Euphrates
Baghdad
Tehran
AFGHANISTAN
Kunlun Moun

Jerusalem
Amman
Mashhad
Kabul
Islamabad
Plateau of Tibet

JORDAN
IRAQ
Kandahar
HIMALAYAS

Syrian Desert
IRAN
Basra
KUWAIT
PAKISTAN
Indus
Delhi

Medina
SAUDI ARABIA
Shiraz
Thar Desert
New Delhi
NEPAL
Mount Eve

Jedda
BAHRAIN
The Gulf
Kathmandu
BHU

Mecca
Riyadh
QATAR
Abu Dhabi
Ganges

UNITED ARAB EMIRATES
Muscat
Karachi
Varanasi
BANGLADESH

Red Sea
Rub al Khali
(Empty Quarter)
OMAN
Dhaka

Sana
Nagpur
Kolkata
(Calcutta)

YEMEN
Arabian Sea
Mumbai
(Bombay)
INDIA

Aden
Socotra
(Yemen)
Bay
Ber

Giant pandas live in bamboo forests in the high mountains of west China. These days, there are fewer than 1,000 giant pandas left in the wild.

Bangalore
Chennai
(Madras)

Cape Comorin
SRI LANKA
Colombo
Sri Jayewardenepura Kotte

MALDIVES
Male

Internet link

For links to websites where you can print out maps of Asia and try an online map quiz, go to
www.usborne-quicklinks.com

Equator

INDIAN OCEAN

East
Siberian
Sea

Laptev
Sea

Anadyr

Bering Sea

Arctic Circle

Verkhoyansk Range

Lena

Okhotsk

Kamchatka
Peninsula

Petropavlovsk-
Kamchatskiy

Yakutsk

Sea of
Okhotsk

eria

Lena

Amur

Komsomolsk

Hokkaido

Sapporo

Lake Baikal

Qiqihar

Sea of
Japan

JAPAN

Tokyo

kutsk

Ulan Bator

MONGOLIA

Shenyang

NORTH
KOREA

Pyongyang

Osaka

Honshu

Gobi Desert

Beijing

Seoul

SOUTH
KOREA

Hiroshima

Baotou

Yellow

Xian

Shanghai

East China

Sea

Tropic of Cancer

CHINA

Hangzhou

Chongqing

Yangtze

Fuzhou

Taipei

TAIWAN

PACIFIC

Kunming

Xianggang (Hong Kong)

Luzon

OCEAN

w

Hainan

PHILIPPINES

RMA
NMAR)

LAOS

Hanoi

Vientiane

South China

Manila

angoon

Sea

Philippine Sea

THAILAND

VIETNAM

angkok

CAMBODIA

Mindanao

Phnom
Penh

Ho Chi Minh City
(Saigon)

Davao

Equator

BRUNEI

MALAYSIA

Kuala Lumpur

New Guinea

dan

SINGAPORE

Borneo

Celebes

Palembang

INDONESIA

Banda Sea

Sumatra

Java Sea

Ujung Pandang

Dili

Arafura Sea

Jakarta

Surabaya

EAST TIMOR

Java

Timor Sea

The white ridges across
the middle of this satellite
photograph of Asia are
the snowy mountaintops
of the Himalayas.

Asia facts

Total land area
*44,537,920km²
(17,196,090 sq miles)*

Biggest country Russia
*Total area: 17,075,200km²
(6,592,735 sq miles) Asiatic Russia:
12,780,800km² (4,934,667 sq miles)*

Smallest country Maldives
300km² (116 sq miles)

Biggest island Borneo
751,100km² (290,000 sq miles)

Highest mountain Mount
Everest, Nepal/China *8,850m
(29,035ft)*

Longest river Yangtze
(Chang Jiang), China *6,380km
(3,964 miles)*

Biggest lake Caspian Sea,
western Asia *370,999km²
(143,243 sq miles)*

Highest waterfall Jog Falls, India
253m (830ft)

Biggest desert Arabian Desert
(deserts of Saudi Arabia)
2,230,000km² (900,000 sq miles)

All kinds of land

Asia has almost every kind of landscape you can think of. In the north, there are freezing forests. To the south, there are deserts and rainforests. Much of central Asia is covered in grassland.

Rice terraces

Some parts of Asia are very hilly. Farmers there make flat shelves called terraces in the land, to grow their crops on. The terraces stop water from running away down the slope, so the rice can grow. Many Asian farmers grow rice in this way.

These hillside terraces make flat areas for rice crops to grow.

High mountains

The highest mountains in the world are the Himalayas. They run through India, Nepal, Bhutan and China. The tallest peak is Mount Everest. Each year, many climbers try to reach the top.

This photograph shows the top, or summit, of Mount Everest. Strong winds are blowing snow off the top.

Rainy seasons

India has two main seasons. One is very rainy, and the other is very dry. These changing seasons are caused by the way the wind blows, and are called monsoons. The monsoons affect when crops can grow.

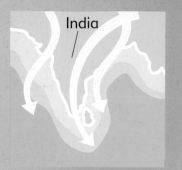

India

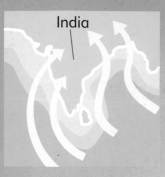

India

In winter, monsoon winds blow from the land out to sea. This is the dry season.

In summer, monsoon winds blow in from the sea, bringing rain. This is the wet season.

Great Wall of China

The people of China built an amazing wall hundreds of years ago, to protect their country from enemies. The Great Wall of China passes through deserts, mountains and grasslands along the northern edge of China. It is so long, it can be seen from space.

Internet link

For links to websites where you can climb Mount Everest, build a rice paddy and explore the Great Wall, go to **www.usborne-quicklinks.com**

The Great Wall of China is made of stone. These watch-towers helped soldiers see their enemies coming.

Many ways of life

Some areas of Asia have hardly any people living in them, but others are very crowded. People across Asia have lots of different beliefs and customs. Ancient traditions often survive alongside modern ways of life.

Tallest buildings

The tallest buildings in the world are the Petronas Towers in Kuala Lumpur, the capital city of Malaysia. They are 452m (1,438ft) high, and have 88 floors, which are used for offices.

This market trader is taking fresh vegetables to sell at the floating market near Bangkok, in Thailand.

The Petronas Towers are much taller than other skyscrapers nearby.

Floating market

Every morning, small boats filled with fruit and vegetables form a floating market on a stretch of canal, near Bangkok in Thailand. Market traders paddle along the canal, selling food and souvenirs to local people and tourists.

Crowded country

China has the biggest population of any country. Over one-fifth of all the people in the world live there. Most of them live in big cities, though. In some parts of China, there are no people at all.

Internet link

For links to websites where you can take photo tours of some of the countries in Asia, go to **www.usborne-quicklinks.com**

Key
people in each km²
(0.39 sq miles)

○ None (deserts)

○ Fewer than 1

○ Up to 100

● More than 100

This map shows where most people live in China.

Glittering spires

Many of the world's religions started in Asia. Buddhism began in India and spread to other Asian countries, including Burma. There are many Buddhist temples in Burma. They are often decorated with pointed spires and large gold statues.

These golden spires are part of a Buddhist temple in Mandalay, Burma.

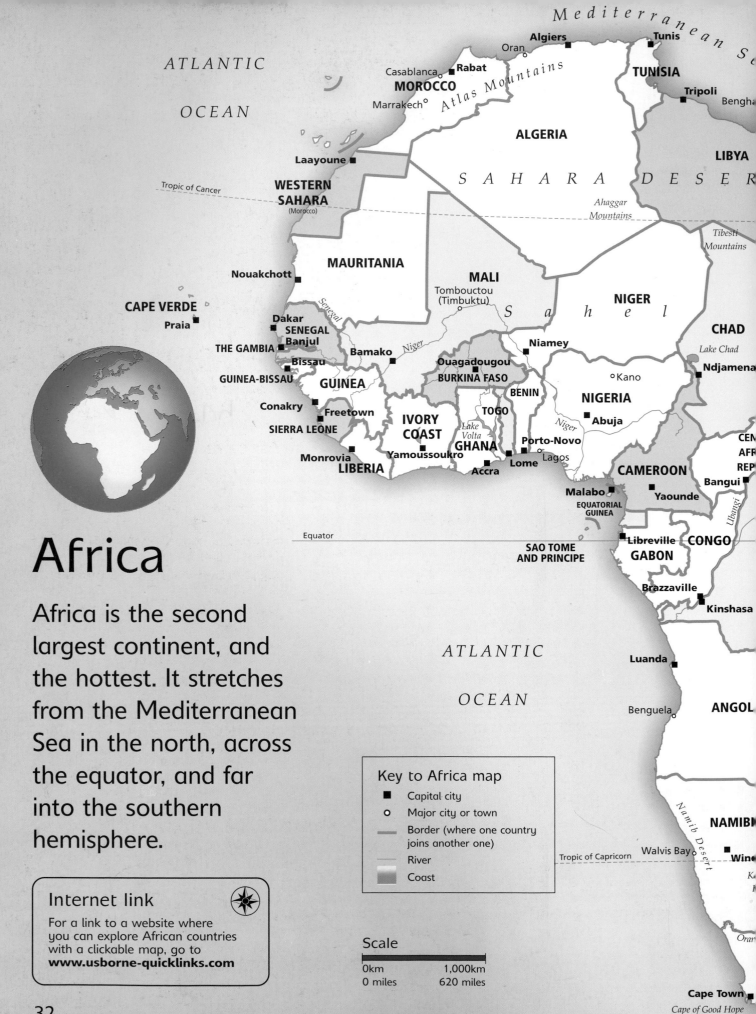

Africa

Africa is the second largest continent, and the hottest. It stretches from the Mediterranean Sea in the north, across the equator, and far into the southern hemisphere.

Internet link

For a link to a website where you can explore African countries with a clickable map, go to **www.usborne-quicklinks.com**

Map labels

Mediterranean Sea

ATLANTIC OCEAN

Algiers
Oran
Tunis
Casablanca
Rabat
TUNISIA
Tripoli
Bengha
MOROCCO
Atlas Mountains
Marrakech
ALGERIA
LIBYA
Laayoune
Tropic of Cancer
WESTERN SAHARA
(Morocco)
S A H A R A   D E S E R
Ahaggar Mountains
Tibesti Mountains
MAURITANIA
MALI
Tombouctou (Timbuktu)
NIGER
S a h e l
CHAD
Nouakchott
Lake Chad
CAPE VERDE
Praia
Dakar
Senegal
SENEGAL
Banjul
Niamey
Ndjamena
THE GAMBIA
Bamako
Niger
Ouagadougou
BURKINA FASO
Kano
Bissau
GUINEA-BISSAU
GUINEA
BENIN
NIGERIA
Conakry
TOGO
Abuja
Freetown
Lake Volta
IVORY COAST
GHANA
Niger
SIERRA LEONE
Yamoussoukro
Porto-Novo
Lagos
Monrovia
Accra
Lome
CEM AFR REP
LIBERIA
CAMEROON
Bangui
Malabo
Yaounde
EQUATORIAL GUINEA
Equator
Ubangi
SAO TOME AND PRINCIPE
Libreville
CONGO
GABON
Brazzaville
Kinshasa
ATLANTIC OCEAN
Luanda
Benguela
ANGOL
Namib Desert
NAMIBI
Tropic of Capricorn
Walvis Bay
Wind
Oran
Cape Town
Cape of Good Hope

Key to Africa map
- ■ Capital city
- ○ Major city or town
- — Border (where one country joins another one)
- — River
- Coast

Scale

0km	1,000km
0 miles	620 miles

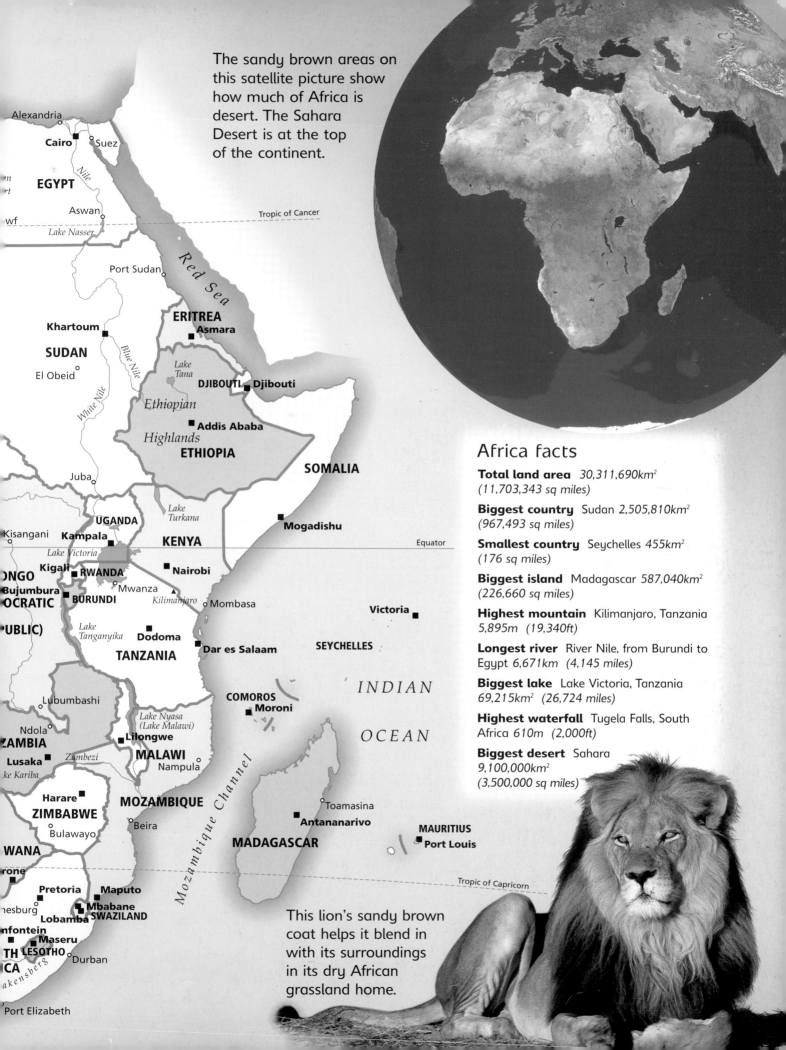

The sandy brown areas on this satellite picture show how much of Africa is desert. The Sahara Desert is at the top of the continent.

Alexandria
Cairo
Suez
Nile
EGYPT
Aswan
Tropic of Cancer
Lake Nasser
wf
Red Sea
Port Sudan
ERITREA
Asmara
Khartoum
Blue Nile
SUDAN
Lake Tana
El Obeid
DJIBOUTI
Djibouti
White Nile
Ethiopian
Addis Ababa
Highlands
ETHIOPIA
Juba
SOMALIA
Lake Turkana
UGANDA
Kisangani
Kampala
Mogadishu
Equator
KENYA
Lake Victoria
Kigali
RWANDA
Nairobi
ONGO
Bujumbura
Mwanza
OCRATIC
BURUNDI
Kilimanjaro
Mombasa
PUBLIC)
Lake Tanganyika
Dodoma
Victoria
TANZANIA
Dar es Salaam
SEYCHELLES
Lubumbashi
INDIAN
COMOROS
Moroni
Ndola
Lake Nyasa (Lake Malawi)
ZAMBIA
Lilongwe
OCEAN
Lusaka
Zambezi
MALAWI
ke Kariba
Nampula
Harare
MOZAMBIQUE
Toamasina
ZIMBABWE
Antananarivo
Bulawayo
Beira
MAURITIUS
WANA
MADAGASCAR
Port Louis
rone
Tropic of Capricorn
Pretoria
Maputo
Mbabane
This lion's sandy brown coat helps it blend in with its surroundings in its dry African grassland home.
Lobamba
SWAZILAND
nesburg
nfontein
Maseru
TH LESOTHO
ICA
Durban
akensberg
Port Elizabeth

Africa facts

Total land area 30,311,690km² *(11,703,343 sq miles)*

Biggest country Sudan 2,505,810km² *(967,493 sq miles)*

Smallest country Seychelles 455km² *(176 sq miles)*

Biggest island Madagascar 587,040km² *(226,660 sq miles)*

Highest mountain Kilimanjaro, Tanzania 5,895m *(19,340ft)*

Longest river River Nile, from Burundi to Egypt 6,671km *(4,145 miles)*

Biggest lake Lake Victoria, Tanzania 69,215km² *(26,724 miles)*

Highest waterfall Tugela Falls, South Africa 610m *(2,000ft)*

Biggest desert Sahara 9,100,000km² *(3,500,000 sq miles)*

Vast desert

A large part of Africa is covered by the Sahara, the biggest desert in the world. It's very hot there during the day, but at night the temperature often drops below freezing.

Dry desert

Hardly any rain falls in the Sahara Desert. The driest part is in Libya, where the desert is sandy. The wind blows the sand into huge piles called dunes, that form dramatic, curving shapes.

Internet link

For links to websites where you can go on a photo safari in Africa and see pictures and facts about the Namib Desert, go to **www.usborne-quicklinks.com**

One of the best ways to cross the Sahara Desert is by camel. Camels can go a long time without water.

This map shows the different kinds of landscapes in Africa.

Sahara Desert

Key

- Highlands
- Scrub
- Desert
- Rainforest
- Savannah grasslands

Thick rainforest

Some places in Africa have plenty of rain. The island of Madagascar is covered in thick, green rainforest. Many unusual animals, such as small, furry lemurs, live there.

Grassy plains

Large parts of Africa are hot grasslands called savannah. It's too dry there for many trees to grow, but there is enough rain for grasses. Savannah animals include lions, giraffes, elephants and zebras.

Ring-tailed lemurs live in the rainforests of Madagascar.

These zebras live in the savannah grasslands. The distant mountain is Kilimanjaro.

Farms and cities

Many people in Africa live in villages and work on farms. But now more and more people are moving to big cities to work and live.

This map shows the farming areas of Africa.

This is the Sahara Desert. No crops can grow here.

Thick rainforest

Key

 Farmland for crops and animals

Land not used for farming

This Zulu woman is carrying water in a clay pot.

Not enough water

Many parts of Africa don't get much rain. When there is too little rain, crops can't grow and people don't have enough water. This is called a drought. Sometimes, water may be carried or brought in pipes to a village where there is a drought.

Internet link

For a link to a website where you can go on a treasure hunt with a secret map of Africa, go to **www.usborne-quicklinks.com**

Farming for money

There are farms in most parts of Africa. Some grow grains such as corn or millet for people living nearby to eat. Others grow crops such as coffee or cocoa, to sell to other countries.

Selling crops is a good way for a country to make money. But it may mean that the people can't grow enough food to eat themselves.

This man is picking tea in Burundi. The dried leaves will be sold to countries far away.

Growing city

Cape Town is one of the three capital cities of South Africa. It is built on flat land, close to the Atlantic Ocean, around the base of Table Mountain. Cape Town is a growing city. More and more people are moving there from the countryside to find better places to live and work.

This is Cape Town, in South Africa. The nearby mountain is covered in cloud.

37

Europe

Europe is a small continent, but it has many countries in it. Only the part of Russia west of the Ural Mountains is in Europe – the rest is in Asia.

Europe is home to many types of birds, such as this common European kingfisher.

ARCTIC OCEAN

Reykjavik
ICELAND

Norwegian Sea

SWEDEN

NORWAY

Bergen

Oslo

Stockholm
Lake Vaner

Gothenburg

British Isles

Edinburgh

Belfast

North Sea

DENMARK
Copenhagen

Baltic

Gdar

IRELAND

Dublin

UNITED KINGDOM

Cardiff
London

ATLANTIC

OCEAN

English Channel

Amsterdam
Hamburg

NETHERLANDS
The Hague

Brussels

Berlin

POLA

BELGIUM

Rhine

GERMANY

Elbe

Oda

LUXEMBOURG
Luxembourg

Prague

CZECH REPUBLIC

Paris

Nantes

Seine

Loire

Danube
Munich

Vienna

Brati

Bay of Biscay

Bordeaux

FRANCE

Bern
LIECHTENSTEIN

SWITZERLAND
Vaduz

Lyon
The Alps

Milan

AUSTRIA

Budap

SLOVENIA
Ljubljana

Zagre

CROATIA

Turin

Po

BOSNIA A
HERZEGOV

Sarajev

Bilbao

Oporto

Andorra la Vella

ANDORRA

MONACO

Marseille

SAN MARINO

Adriatic Sea

PORTUGAL

Madrid

Barcelona

Corsica (France)

ITALY

Lisbon

Tagus

SPAIN

Valencia

Rome **VATICAN CITY**

AL
T

Cordoba

Naples

Gibraltar (U.K.)

Sardinia (Italy)

Mediterranean Sea

Sicily (Italy)

MALTA **Valletta**

Key to Europe map

- ■ Capital city
- ○ Major city or town
- Border (where one country joins another one)
- River
- Coast

Scale

0km — 500km
0 miles — 310 miles

North Cape

Barents Sea

The rest
of Russia
is in Asia.

Arctic Circle

Murmansk

*Kola
Peninsula*

land

Pechora

Ukhta

Oulu

Arkhangelsk

Northern Dvina

FINLAND

Lake Onega

U r a l   M o u n t a i n s

R U S S I A

Perm

Lake Ladoga

ɨnki

St. Petersburg

Cherepovets

*Rybinsk
Reservoir*

Volga

Kama

Tallinn

ESTONIA

Nizhniy Novgorod

Kazan

Riga

LATVIA

Moscow

Samara

THUANIA

Vilnius

Tula

Don

Volga

Minsk

BELARUS

aw

Voronezh

Kiev

Kharkiv

Volgograd

chula

w

Dnieper

Volga

Lviv

UKRAINE

Donetsk

Don

Astrakhan

VAKIA

Dnipropetrovsk

Rostov

Carpathian Mountains

MOLDOVA

GARY

Chisinau

Odesa

*Sea of
Azov*

*Caspian
Sea*

Cluj-Napoca

*Crimean
Peninsula*

ROMANIA

Caucasus Mountains

rade

Bucharest

▲
Mount Elbrus

Danube

Black Sea

A AND

NEGRO

BULGARIA

Sofia

Skopje

CEDONIA

ECE

*Aegean
Sea*

ECE

Athens

Crete
(Greece)

This satellite photograph
shows how Europe joins
onto Asia. The big, white
patch at the top is the ice
that covers the Arctic.

Europe facts

Total land area *10,205,720km²
(3,940,428 sq miles)*

Biggest country Russia
*Total area: 17,075,200km²
(6,492,735 sq miles)
Area of European Russia:
4,294,400km² (658,068 sq miles)*

Smallest country Vatican City
0.44km² (0.17 sq miles)

Biggest island Great Britain
229,870km² (90,506 sq miles)

Highest mountain Mount Elbrus,
Russia *5,642m (18,510ft)*

Longest river Volga *3,700km
(2,298 miles)*

Biggest lake Lake Ladoga, Russia
17,700km² (6,834 sq miles)

Highest waterfall Utigard, on
the Jostedal Glacier, Norway
800m (2,625ft)

Biggest desert There are no
deserts in Europe.

Internet link

For links to websites where you
can print out maps of Europe, and
play activities and games, go to
www.usborne-quicklinks.com

Farms and hills

A lot of the land in Europe is gently hilly and good for farming. Some areas are rocky or snowy, and fewer crops grow there.

This map shows some of the crops that grow in Europe.

Key

○ Grapes

○ Olives (for oil)

● Fruit

● Potatoes

○ Grains, such as wheat and barley

Europe

Asia

Mediterranean Sea

Fruit and vegetables

The south of Europe is on the coast of the Mediterranean Sea. The weather there is very hot and dry in summer, but cool and wet in winter. Oranges, lemons and other citrus fruits grow well there, as well as many other kinds of fruit and vegetables.

This market is in Rome, in Italy. Every day, people bring fresh fruit and vegetables from the farms nearby, to sell at the market.

Natural hot water

The island of Iceland has natural hot water, heated by rocks under the Earth. From time to time, jets of steam and hot water burst out through holes in the ground. These jets are called geysers.

This is Strokkur Geyser, in Iceland. Boiling hot water erupts from it every few minutes.

Jagged peaks

The largest group of mountains in Europe is the Alps. They formed millions of years ago, out of giant folds of rock. They have very jagged shapes, which were carved out by rivers of ice, called glaciers.

This picture shows how some of the valleys and lower slopes of the Alps are used for farming crops. Behind, you can see much higher, snowy peaks.

Internet link

For links to websites where you can find out more about European countries with jigsaws and flag games, go to **www.usborne-quicklinks.com**

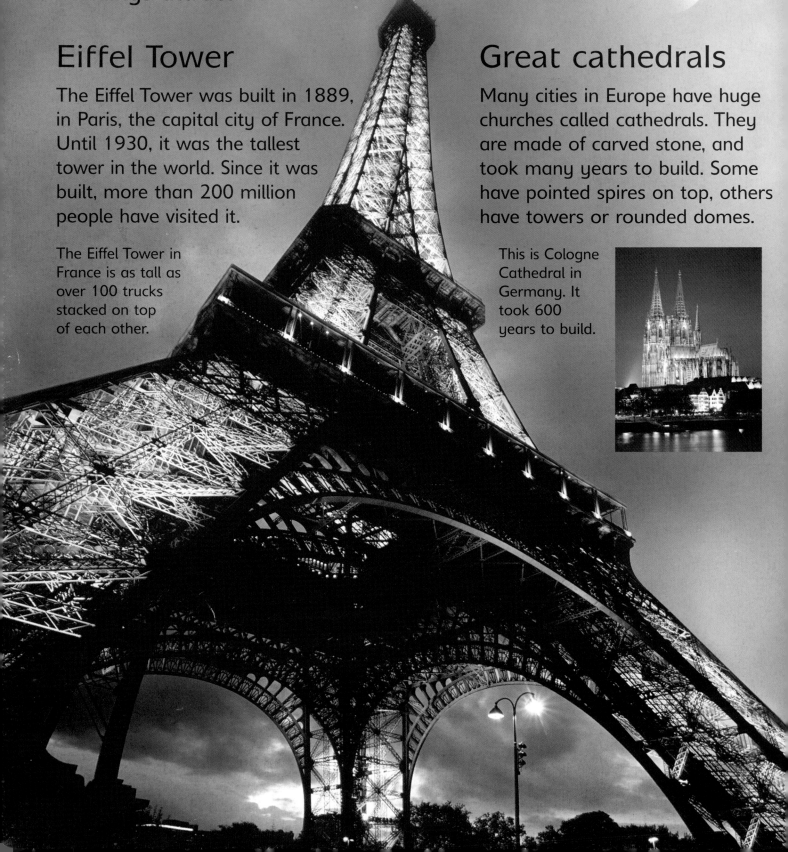

Places to see

Europe is famous for its beautiful old cities and historic buildings. But many exciting modern buildings attract visitors too.

Eiffel Tower

The Eiffel Tower was built in 1889, in Paris, the capital city of France. Until 1930, it was the tallest tower in the world. Since it was built, more than 200 million people have visited it.

The Eiffel Tower in France is as tall as over 100 trucks stacked on top of each other.

Great cathedrals

Many cities in Europe have huge churches called cathedrals. They are made of carved stone, and took many years to build. Some have pointed spires on top, others have towers or rounded domes.

This is Cologne Cathedral in Germany. It took 600 years to build.

Modern buildings

There are some amazing modern buildings in Europe.
One of the most interesting is Spain's Museo Guggenheim
Bilbao. It is covered with huge curving sheets of metal.

This is the Museo Guggenheim Bilbao in Spain. It is a gallery where people go to look at modern art.

Roman remains

About 2,000 years ago, Rome was
one of the biggest cities in the world.
At that time, the Romans ruled all the
lands around the Mediterranean Sea.
Ruins of Roman buildings can still be
seen in lots of places in Europe.

Internet link

For links to websites where you can visit the
Eiffel Tower, and print out models of famous
buildings, go to **www.usborne-quicklinks.com**

This map shows where
the Romans ruled in
Europe. These lands
were called the
Roman Empire.

These are the remains of the Colosseum in Rome.
People came here to see fighters called gladiators.

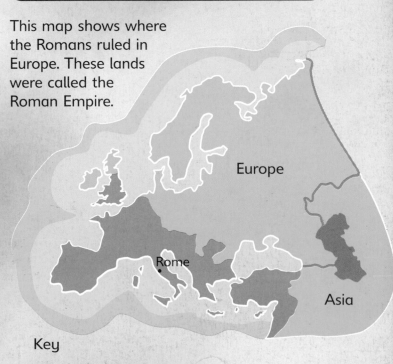

Europe

Rome

Asia

Key

The Roman Empire

Oceania

Oceania is the smallest continent. It is made up of Australia, New Zealand and Papua New Guinea, as well as many smaller islands dotted across the Pacific Ocean.

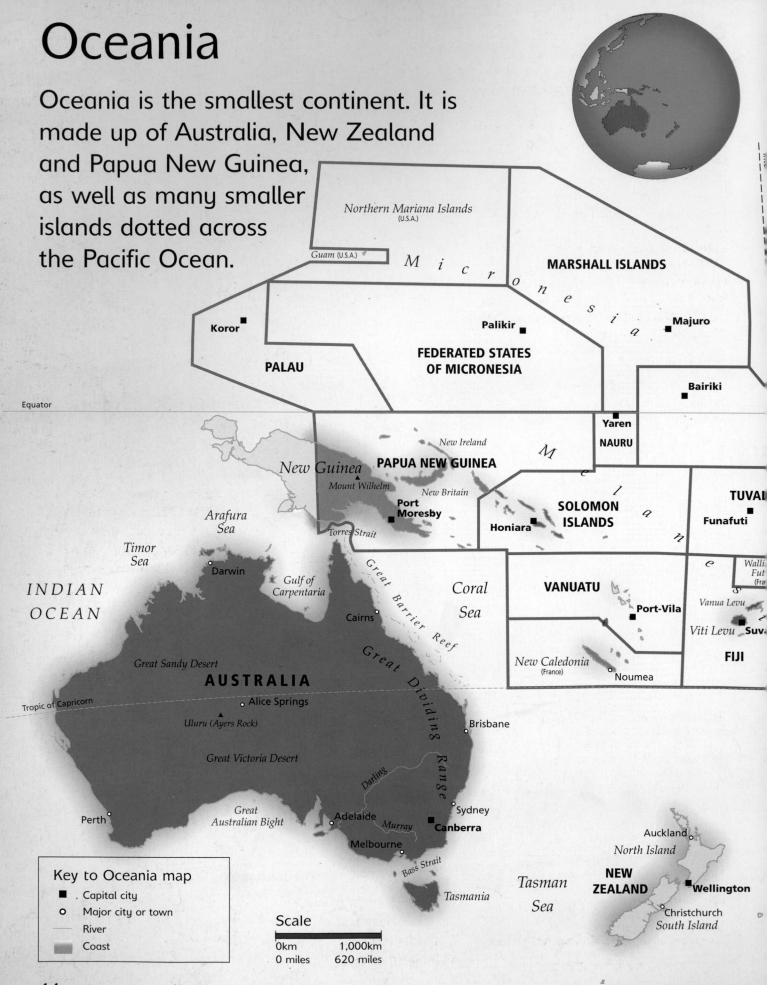

Northern Mariana Islands (U.S.A.)

Guam (U.S.A.)

Micronesia

MARSHALL ISLANDS

Koror ■

Palikir ■

Majuro ■

PALAU

FEDERATED STATES OF MICRONESIA

Bairiki ■

Equator

Yaren ■
NAURU

New Ireland

PAPUA NEW GUINEA

Melanesia

New Guinea

Mount Wilhelm ▲

New Britain

SOLOMON ISLANDS

TUVAL

Funafuti ■

Arafura Sea

Port Moresby ■

Honiara ■

Torres Strait

Timor Sea

Darwin ○

Gulf of Carpentaria

VANUATU

Coral Sea

Walli Fut (Fra)

INDIAN OCEAN

Cairns ○

Great Barrier Reef

Port-Vila ■

Vanua Levu

Viti Levu **Suva**

FIJI

Great Sandy Desert

AUSTRALIA

New Caledonia (France)

Noumea ○

Tropic of Capricorn

Alice Springs ○

Uluru (Ayers Rock) ▲

Brisbane ○

Great Victoria Desert

Darling

Great Dividing Range

Perth ○

Great Australian Bight

Adelaide ○

Murray

Sydney ○

■ **Canberra**

Melbourne ○

Auckland ○

North Island

Bass Strait

NEW ZEALAND

■ Wellington

Tasmania

Tasman Sea

Christchurch ○
South Island

Key to Oceania map
- ■ Capital city
- ○ Major city or town
- — River
- Coast

Scale

0km   1,000km
0 miles   620 miles

44

Oceania facts

Total land area 8,564,400km² (3,306,715 sq miles)

Biggest country Australia 7,741,220km² (2,988,885 sq miles)

Smallest country Nauru 21km² (8 sq miles)

Biggest island New Guinea 800,000km² (309,000 sq miles)

Highest mountain Mount Wilhelm, Papua New Guinea 4,509m (14,793ft)

Longest river Murray/Darling River Australia 3,718km (2,310 miles)

Biggest lake Lake Eyre, Australia 9,000km² (3,470 sq miles)

Highest waterfall Sutherland Falls on the Arthur River, New Zealand 580m (1,904ft)

Biggest desert Great Victoria Desert, Australia 388,500km² (150,000 sq miles)

Polynesia

KIRIBATI

Tokelau (New Zealand)

MOA
pia

American Samoa (U.S.A.)

GA

lofa

Niue (New Zealand)

Cook Islands (New Zealand)

Tahiti

French Polynesia (France)

Equator

PACIFIC OCEAN

Tropic of Capricorn

Pitcairn Islands (U.K.)

Date Line

Some of the countries in Oceania are made up of hundreds of islands, which are too small to be seen on this map. The red lines show where one country ends and another begins.

This photograph was taken from space. The light brown areas show that much of Australia is desert. The large, white area below Australia is Antarctica.

Wallabies live in the dry, dusty grasslands of Australia. Their long eyelashes protect their eyes from blowing sand.

Internet links

For links to websites where you can take a virtual trip of Australia and print out maps, go to **www.usborne-quicklinks.com**

Desert and ocean

Oceania is made up of over 20,000 islands in the Pacific Ocean. Most of them are tiny, but the desert land of Australia is huge. Many small islands are the tops of underwater volcanoes.

The deepest place

The bottom of the Pacific Ocean is covered in mountains, and valleys called trenches. The deepest place on Earth is in the Mariana Trench. It is over 11km (6.8 miles) deep. If you dropped a small rock into the sea, it would take over an hour to reach the bottom of the Mariana Trench.

These maps show the Mariana Trench and the Challenger Deep, which is its deepest part.

Japan (Asia)

Philippines (Asia)

Mariana Islands

Mariana Islands (enlarged)

Guam

Key

Islands

● Trench

● Challenger Deep

Ancient land

Most of Australia is a bare, rocky desert. Its land has hardly changed for millions of years. The rocks have slowly been worn into smooth shapes by the wind and rain.

Wave Rock in Australia looks like a towering wall of water. It was worn into this unusual shape by the wind and rain.

Internet link

For a link to explore the Great Barrier coral reef off the coast of Australia, go to **www.usborne-quicklinks.com**

How islands form

The oldest islands in Oceania are made of limestone rock. The youngest islands are the tips of underwater volcanoes. These pictures show how an island forms and changes.

A volcano grows under the sea and rises up above the surface. When it stops erupting, animals and plants live on it.

Sea animals called corals grow around the edge of the dead volcano. They form a ring of coral called an atoll.

The coral dies and forms hard limestone. Forests grow on these new islands. The soft rock of the volcano is slowly worn away by the sea.

The middle part of this island in French Polynesia is a volcano. It is surrounded by coral reefs, which are large areas of tiny sea animals called corals.

Forests by the sea

Mangrove trees live on the edge of warm seas, with their roots partly underwater. Unlike most plants, they aren't harmed by salty sea water. Thick mangrove forests grow in Papua New Guinea and other islands in Oceania.

The roots of mangrove trees spread out wide and prop the trees up in the swampy ground.

Ocean living

Fewer people live in Oceania than on any other continent apart from Antarctica. Most of Oceania's people live near the sea.

Australia's people

Four out of five Australians live in towns and cities that are within one hour's drive of the sea. The rest live scattered across the huge desert area called the outback. People there live so far apart that some children have to do their schoolwork by mail or over the Internet.

This map shows how many people live in different parts of Australia.

Most Australians live near the sea, and many enjoy water sports. This man has found a good wave to surf, near a beach in Australia.

Original people

Most people in Australia and New Zealand today are related to people who came from Europe. But the first people in Australia were the Aboriginal people, thousands of years before. The first settlers in New Zealand were the Maoris.

Key
people in each km² (0.39 sq miles)

- ● More than 50
- ● 4–50
- ● 2–4
- ● 1 – 2
- ● Fewer than 1

These men are wearing traditional Maori costumes. All children in New Zealand learn about Maori traditions at school.

Internet link

For links to websites with photo galleries of the Pacific islands and fun facts about Australia, go to **www.usborne-quicklinks.com**

Fiji's farmers

Many Fijians are farmers. They grow enough food, such as corn and vegetables, for their families and other people in their villages. Some of their crops, such as coconuts and sugar cane, are sold to other countries.

Farming people on Fiji often live in one-room houses like these, with thatched roofs and woven floor mats inside.

Dressing up

The Huli people live in the mountains of Papua New Guinea. Huli men paint their faces and dress in spectacular feathered wigs to perform dances, which are famous all over the world.

This Huli man is putting on face paint. His wig is made from grasses, and feathers from a bird called a cassowary.

The Arctic

The area around the North Pole is called the Arctic. There's no land at the North Pole, but the sea there is so cold that its surface freezes and turns to thick ice.

The white patch on this globe shows the parts of the Arctic that are always covered with ice.

Frozen land

The Arctic Circle is an imaginary line around the Arctic. Eight countries have land inside the Arctic Circle. This land is called tundra. The soil there is frozen for most of the year. No trees can grow, but lichen and moss plants grow close to the ground.

Internet link

For a link to a website where you can take part in a quiz about animals that live in the Arctic, go to **www.usborne-quicklinks.com**

Coping with cold

Arctic animals have to survive freezing temperatures. Many have thick, bushy white coats to keep them warm and help them blend in with the snow. Some have a layer of fat for extra warmth.

This baby harp seal has thick fur, and a layer of fat under its skin to keep it warm.

Scale

0km   1,000km
0 miles   620 miles

PACIFIC

OCEAN

Aleutian Islands

Bering
Sea

○ Anchorage

ALASKA
(U.S.A.)

Arctic Circle

○ Anadyr

RUSSIA

○ Petropavlosk-
Kamchatskiy

JAPAN
● Sapporo

Chukchi
Sea

Wrangel
Island

East
Siberian
Sea

Verkhoyansk Range

Rocky Mountains   *Yukon*

Beaufort
Sea

New
Siberia
Islands

Lena

○ Yellowknife

Victoria
Island

Laptev
Sea

Yenisey

CANADA

Queen
Elizabeth
Islands

North
Magnetic Pole

ARCTIC

Severnaya
Zemlya

+ North Pole

OCEAN

Ellesmere
Island

Kara
Sea

Ob

Baffin
Island

Franz
Josef
Land

Novaya
Zemlya

Ural Mountains

○ Yekaterinburg

Baffin
Bay

Svalbard
(Norway)

RUSSIA

Davis Strait

GREENLAND
(Denmark)

Barents
Sea

● Murmansk

○ Arkhangelsk

Godthab ■

Greenland
Sea

Norwegian
Sea

Arctic Circle

FINLAND

○ Nizhniy
Novgorod

Reykjavik ▪

ICELAND

SWEDEN

■ **Helsinki**

■ **Moscow**

Faroe
Islands
(Denmark)

NORWAY

ESTONIA

Oslo ■   ■ **Stockholm**

LATVIA

ATLANTIC

LITHUANIA

BELARUS

OCEAN

North
Sea

Baltic
Sea

RUSSIA

IRELAND

UNITED
KINGDOM

DENMARK

POLAND

UKRAINE

NETHERLANDS

GERMANY

BELGIUM

CZECH
REPUBLIC

SLOVAKIA

MOLDOVA

ROMANIA

The Antarctic

The Antarctic, also called Antarctica, is the continent at the South Pole. It is the coldest and windiest continent. The land is covered with ice over 2,000m (6,500ft) thick. Nine-tenths of all the world's ice is in the Antarctic.

The Antarctic is at the bottom of the Earth. It is surrounded by the Southern Ocean.

This scientist is studying an ice cave. The cave is in an ice shelf, about 100m (328ft) thick, that floats on the sea.

Home for scientists

People started exploring the Antarctic just over 100 years ago. The only people who live there today are scientists. They study the weather, ice and rocks to try to find out more about life on Earth.

Keeping warm

The Antarctic is home to thousands of penguins. They have layers of fat underneath their feathers to protect them from the cold, and huddle together in big groups for extra warmth. Penguins take turns standing at the edge of the group, where it's windy and much colder.

Internet link

For a link to a website featuring Antarctic maps, satellite views, animals and even jokes go to **www.usborne-quicklinks.com**

South Georgia
(U.K.)

South Sandwich
Islands
(U.K.)

Antarctic Circle

South Orkney Islands
(U.K.)

South Shetland Islands
(U.K.)

Queen Maud Land

*Weddell
Sea*

*Coats
Land*

*Enderby
Land*

*Antarctic
Peninsula*

ANTARCTICA

*East
Antarctica*

*Ronne
Ice Shelf*

*Bellingshausen
Sea*

Vinson Massif
▲
**5,140m
(16,863ft)**

+ South Pole

*Ellsworth
Land*

*West
Antarctica*

Transantarctic Mountains

*Amundsen
Sea*

Marie Byrd Land

Wilkes Land

*Ross
Ice Shelf*

Ross Sea

*Victoria
Land*

South Magnetic
Pole
+

Antarctic Circle

Scale

0km	1,000km
0 miles	620 miles

S O U T H E R N
O C E A N

Key to Antarctic map

▲ Mountain

▬ Coast

This emperor penguin chick is
keeping warm by standing on
its mother's feet and snuggling
up against her tummy.

Flags of the world

North America

Antigua and Barbuda

Bahamas

Barbados

Belize

Canada

Costa Rica

Cuba

Dominica

Dominican Republic

El Salvador

Grenada

Guatemala

Haiti

Honduras

Jamaica

Mexico

Nicaragua

Panama

St. Kitts and Nevis

St. Lucia

St. Vincent and the Grenadines

Trinidad and Tobago

United States of America

South America

Argentina

Bolivia

Brazil

Chile

Colombia

Ecuador

Guyana

Paraguay

Peru

Surinam

Uruguay

Venezuela

Asia

Afghanistan

Armenia

Azerbaijan

Bahrain

Bangladesh

Bhutan

Brunei

Burma (Myanmar)

Cambodia

China

East Timor

Georgia

Asia (continued)

 India

 Indonesia

 Iran

 Iraq

 Israel

 Japan

 Jordan

 Kazakhstan

 Kuwait

 Kyrgyzstan

 Laos

 Lebanon

 Malaysia

 Maldives

 Mongolia

 Nepal

 North Korea

 Oman

 Pakistan

 Philippines

 Qatar

 Russian Federation

 Saudi Arabia

 Singapore

 South Korea

 Sri Lanka

 Syria

 Taiwan

 Tajikistan

 Thailand

 Turkey

 Turkmenistan

 United Arab Emirates

 Uzbekistan

 Vietnam

 Yemen

Africa

 Algeria

 Angola

 Benin

 Botswana

 Burkina Faso

Burundi

Cameroon

Cape Verde

Central African Republic

Chad

Comoros

Congo

Congo (Democratic Republic)

Djibouti

Egypt

Equatorial Guinea

Eritrea

Ethiopia

Africa (continued)

 Gabon

 The Gambia

 Ghana

 Guinea

 Guinea-Bissau

 Ivory Coast

 Kenya

 Lesotho

 Liberia

 Libya

 Madagascar

 Malawi

 Mali

 Mauritania

 Mauritius

 Morocco

 Mozambique

 Namibia

 Niger

 Nigeria

 Rwanda

 Sao Tome and Principe

 Senegal

 Seychelles

 Sierra Leone

 Somalia

 South Africa

 Sudan

 Swaziland

 Tanzania

 Togo

 Tunisia

 Uganda

 Zambia

 Zimbabwe

Europe

 Albania

 Andorra

 Austria

 Belarus

 Belgium

 Bosnia and Herzegovina

 Bulgaria

 Croatia

 Cyprus

Czech Republic

Denmark

Estonia

Finland

France

Germany

Greece

Hungary

Iceland

Europe (continued)

Ireland

Italy

Latvia

Liechtenstein

Lithuania

Luxembourg

Macedonia

Malta

Moldova

Monaco

Netherlands

Norway

Poland

Portugal

Romania

Russian Federation

San Marino

Serbia and Montenegro

Slovakia

Slovenia

Spain

Sweden

Switzerland

Turkey

Ukraine

United Kingdom

Vatican City

Oceania

Australia

Federated States of Micronesia

Fiji

Kiribati

Marshall Islands

Nauru

New Zealand

Palau

Papua New Guinea

Samoa

Solomon Islands

Tonga

Tuvalu

Vanuatu

Changing flags

Flags of the world change frequently. New flags are invented as new countries are born, or their situation changes.

For example, in 1991, there were important changes to the way South Africa was run. All adults in the country were allowed to vote in free elections for the first time. To celebrate this, a new flag was designed.

New flag of South Africa

South African flag until 1994

Internet links

For a link to a website with flags and facts, go to
www.usborne-quicklinks.com

Map index

This is an index of all the places and features named on the maps. Each entry may contain the following parts: the name of the country, place or feature (in **bold** type), the country or region where a place or feature is (in *italic* type), and the page(s) where it can be found (in plain type). Some names also have a description explaining exactly what kind of place they are, for example, capital cities or rivers.

Index

Acknowledgements

Every effort has been made to trace the copyright holders of the material in this book. If any rights have been omitted, the publishers offer to rectify this in any future edition, following notification. The publishers are grateful to the following organizations and individuals for their contribution and permission to reproduce this material.

Cover (Front) Digital Vision, (back) Digital Vision; **1** NASA/Science Photo Library; **2–3** Getty Images/Pal Hermansen; **5** Getty Images/Walter Bibikow; **7** Getty Images/Louise Murray; **8**(b) Dave G. Houser/CORBIS; **14**(bl) Digital Vision; **15**(tr) Julian Baum & David Angus/Science Photo Library; **16**(l) Getty Images/John Giustina; **16–17** Getty Images/Macduff Everton; **17**(tr) Roger Ressmeyer/CORBIS; **18** Powerstock; **19**(tr) Owaki-Kulla/CORBIS, (l) Bryan & Cherry Alexander Photography/Alamy, (br) Getty Images/Doug Armand; **20**(bl) Digital Vision; **21**(tr) Julian Baum & David Angus/Science Photo Library; **22** Galen Rowell/CORBIS; **23**(tl) Powerstock, (r) Owen Franken/CORBIS, (bl) Robert Harding Picture Library Ltd/Alamy; **24** Jim Zuckerman/Alamy; **25**(r) Robert Harding Picture Library Ltd/Alamy, (l) Getty Images/Ary Diesendruck; **26**(bl) Digital Vision; **27**(tr) Julian Baum & David Angus/Science Photo Library; **28**(l) Jon Arnold Images/Alamy, (br) Michael S. Lewis/CORBIS; **29** Miles Ertman/Masterfile; **30**(main) World Pictures, (bl) Macduff Everton/CORBIS; **31**(br) Powerstock; **33**(tr) Tom Van Sant/Geosphere Project, Santa Monica/Science Photo Library, (br) Digital Vision; **34–35**(b) Getty Images/Frans Lemmens; **35**(tr) Getty Images/Nick Garbutt, (m) NHPA/Daryl Balfour; **36** Dallas and John Heaton/Alamy; **37**(tr) Getty Images/Bruno De Hogues, (bl) Getty Images/Stephen Beer; **38**(ml) Digital Vision; **39**(br) Julian Baum & David Angus/Science Photo Library; **40**(bl) Art Kowalsky/Alamy; **40–41**(main) Jon Arnold Images/ Alamy; **41**(mr) Getty Images/Wilfried Krecichwost; **42**(main) Getty Images/John Lawrence, (mr) Getty Images/ Jorg Greuel; **43**(t) Powerstock, (bl) Getty Images/A & L Sinibaldi; **45**(t) Planetary Visions Ltd/Science Photo Library, (b) Digital Vision; **46**(b) Jean Paul Ferrero/Ardea London Ltd; **47**(t) Tim McKenna/CORBIS, (br) Theo Allofs/CORBIS; **48**(t) Mark A. Johnson/CORBIS, (br) Anders Ryman/CORBIS; **49**(ml) Jon Arnold Images/Alamy, (r) Wolfgang Kaehler/CORBIS; **50**(b) W. Perry Conway/CORBIS; **52** Graham Neden, Ecoscene/CORBIS; **53**(br) Tim David/CORBIS.

American editor: Carrie A. Seay